✦ **Merry Christmas!** ✦

From Redeemer "2003"

First Grade Sunday School Teachers

Jesus Loves You And We Do Too!

Mr. Brian, Ms. Holly, Mr. Jeff & Mr. Jim

The Standard Publishing Company, Cincinnati, Ohio.
A division of Standex International Corporation.
© 1997 by The Standard Publishing Company. All rights reserved.
Printed in the United States of America.
Library of Congress Card Catalog Number 96-070323.
04 03 02 01 00 99 98 97   5 4 3 2 1

Scripture in this book is from the International Children's Bible,
New Century Version, © 1986, 1988 by Word Publishing,
Dallas, Texas 75039. Used by permission.

Designed by Coleen Davis
Edited by Greg Holder

My Bible Pals

THINGS TO KNOW

by Clare Mishica

illustrated by Jodie McCallum

STANDARD
PUBLISHING
Cincinnati, Ohio

TRAVEL

boat

wagon

chariot

camel

luggage

donkey

cart

walking

Mary and Joseph Come to Bethlehem

Mary and Joseph had traveled from Nazareth to the town of Bethlehem. The trip was hard on Mary because she was almost ready to have a baby!

But Bethlehem was very busy! Wherever Mary and Joseph tried to rent a room, the innkeeper would say, "Sorry, but we are all filled up!"

Finally, one innkeeper felt sorry for them. He said, "I don't have any rooms for you, but you are welcome to sleep in my stable with the animals. Mary and Joseph were very grateful, and were soon settled into the stable.

That night, Mary gave birth to a baby boy. They named him "Jesus." But this was a very special baby. Jesus was the Son of God!

How many camels do you see?
Can you find Hideaway Mouse?

HOUSES

Healing the Paralyzed Man

A man who could not walk heard about Jesus. "Jesus can make sick people well," he told his friends. "I must see him."

The friends carried the man on his bed to a house. Jesus was inside the house, but they could not get inside. The house was too full of people!

The friends had an idea. They climbed the steps up to the roof. Then they made a hole and lowered the man right down through the roof!

Jesus smiled at the man. "Get up and walk," he said.

The man stood up! He could walk like everybody else!

Everyone was amazed, especially the man's friends.

Which part of the house begins with the letter "R"?
Where is Hideaway Mouse?

broom

stairway

roll-up mat

dirt floor

roof

clay wall

pitcher

basin

oven

bushel

fire pit

Dinner at Zacchaeus' House

Zacchaeus was a little man who cheated everyone. He would always charge people more money than they really owed him.

One day, Jesus came to the town where Zacchaeus lived. People rushed to see him. Zacchaeus wanted to see Jesus, too. But a big crowd stood in his way.

Then Zacchaeus found a big tree to climb. When he reached the top, he looked down at the crowd. He could see Jesus!

"Come down, Zacchaeus," said Jesus. "I will stay at your house today."

Zacchaeus couldn't believe it! He quickly came down out of the tree! He was so excited! He couldn't stop smiling.

Zacchaeus took Jesus to his home. "I'm sorry for cheating people," Zacchaeus said. "I'll pay back all the money I stole."

Jesus smiled. Zacchaeus was finally doing the right thing.

Find the square in this picture.
Can you find Hideaway Mouse?

cucumbers

grapes

salted fish

bread

honey

Parable of the Lost Sheep

Once, Jesus told a crowd of people this story:

Late one night, a shepherd was counting his sheep. ". . 97, 98, 99. Oh, no!" the shepherd cried. "One lamb is lost! I must find it!"

The shepherd looked everywhere for the little lamb. He finally found him trapped in a rocky cave. The lamb was alone and very frightened.

Carefully, the shepherd rescued the little lamb from the cave. He joyfully carried the lamb home on his shoulders.

That night, the happy shepherd woke up all his friends. "Let's celebrate!" he shouted. "I found my lost lamb!"

ANIMALS

lion

ox

donkey

bear

fox

fish

When Jesus finished the story, he said, "When we disobey God, we are like the lost lamb. But God is happy when we are sorry. He is like the shepherd who found his lamb."

How many sheep can you count?
Where is Hideaway Mouse?

PLAYTIME

Jesus and the Children

Mommies and daddies carried their babies down the dusty road. Little boys and girls came along, too. They were all going to see Jesus.

But Jesus' friends stopped them. "You cannot see Jesus now," they said. "He is too busy for little children."

When Jesus heard this, he was angry. "Do not stop the children," he said. "Let them come to me."

Quickly, a little boy wiggled through the crowd. He jumped into Jesus' arms. Jesus laughed and gave him a hug.

The other children came to Jesus, too. He hugged and blessed them all. Jesus loved little children very much.

What games begins with the letter "H"?
Can you find Hideaway Mouse?

doll

wrestling

tops

marbles

ball

hoops

hopscotch

whistle

make-believe wedding

JOBS

Jesus Calls the Fishermen

Jesus was very busy teaching people about God's love. What a big job! He wanted some special friends to help him.

One day, Jesus was standing on the rocky shore by the sea. When he looked out on the water, he spotted Peter and Andrew fishing in their boat. He also saw James and John fixing a hole in their fishing net. Jesus knew the four fishermen would be good helpers.

"Come and follow me," Jesus called.

At once, Peter and Andrew said, "Yes, we will come!"

James and John said, "We will come, too!" and quickly came to shore. They left everything on the beach and followed Jesus.

Find the triangle in this picture.
Where is Hideaway Mouse?

potter

scribe

carpenter

centurion

merchant

tax collector

tentmaker

farmer

CLOTHES

turban

tunic

armor

cloth

sackcloth

robe

sandals

The Story of Dorcas

Once there was a woman named Dorcas. She always tried to help other people. She made warm coats for poor people who couldn't buy them.

But one day, Dorcas got sick and died. Dorcas' friends were very sad. They asked Peter, Jesus' special friend, to come and help her.

"Please help Dorcas," her friends begged Peter. "She was a very good person." Then they showed him the warm coats she had made for them.

Peter knelt by Dorcas. He prayed to Jesus and said, "Dorcas, stand up."

Dorcas' eyes opened. She got up! Jesus had answered Peter's prayer. Dorcas' friends told everybody about the wonderful miracle they had seen.

How many birds do you see in this picture?
Can you find Hideaway Mouse?

Things Every Bible Pal Should Know

Be happy to give and ready to share.
1 Timothy 6:18

Love the Lord your God with all your heart.
Deuteronomy 6:5

Obey your parents.
Ephesians 6:1

Do for other people the same things you want them to do for you.
Matthew 7:12

Forgive each other.
Ephesians 4:32

A friend loves at all times.
Proverbs 17:17